Retrieved Attachments

Peter Robinson was born in Salford, Lancashire, in 1953 and grew up mainly in Liverpool. He holds degrees from the Universities of York and Cambridge. After teaching for many years in Japan, he returned to Europe in 2007 and is currently Professor of English and American Literature at the University of Reading. The poetry editor for Two Rivers Press, author of many books of poems, translations, prose fiction, and literary criticism, he has been awarded the Cheltenham Prize, the John Florio Prize, and two Poetry Book Society Recommendations.

Poetry in translation by Two Rivers Press

Philippe Jaccottet, *In Winter Light* translated by Tim Dooley (2022)
Charles Baudelaire, *Paris Scenes* translated by Ian Brinton (2021)
René Noyau, *Earth on Fire and other Poems* translated
    by Gérard Noyau with Peter Pegnall (2021)
Maria Teresa Horta, *Point of Honour* translated by Lesley Saunders (2019)
Henri Michaux, *Storms under the Skin* translated by Jane Draycott (2017)

Also by Two Rivers poets

William Bedford, *The Dancers of Colbek* (2020)
Kate Behrens, *Penumbra* (2019)
Kate Behrens, *Transitional Spaces* (2022)
Conor Carville, *English Martyrs* (2019)
David Cooke, *Sicilian Elephants* (2021)
Tim Dooley, *Discoveries* (2022)
Jane Draycott, *Tideway* (re-issued 2022)
Claire Dyer, *Yield* (2021)
John Froy, *Sandpaper & Seahorses* (2018)
James Harpur, *The Examined Life* (2021)
Ian House, *Just a Moment* (2020)
Rosie Jackson & Graham Burchell, *Two Girls and a Beehive* (2020)
Gill Learner, *Change* (2021)
Sue Leigh, *Chosen Hill* (2018)
Sue Leigh, *Her Orchards* (2021)
Becci Louise, *Octopus Medicine* (2017)
Steven Matthews, *On Magnetism* (2017)
James Peake, *Reaction Time of Glass* (2019)
James Peake, *The Star in the Branches* (2022)
Peter Robinson & David Inshaw, *Bonjour Mr Inshaw* (2020)
Peter Robinson, *English Nettles* (re-issued 2022)
Lesley Saunders, *Nominy-Dominy* (2018)
Lesley Saunders, *This Thing of Blood & Love* (2022)
Jack Thacker, *Handling* (2018)
Robin Thomas, *The Weather on the Moon* (2022)
Susan Utting, *Half the Human Race* (2017)
Jean Watkins, *Precarious Lives* (2018)

Retrieved Attachments

Peter Robinson

First published in the UK in 2023 by Two Rivers Press
7 Denmark Road, Reading RG1 5PA.
www.tworiverspress.com

© Peter Robinson 2023

The right of the poet to be identified as the author of this work
has been asserted by him in accordance with the Copyright, Designs
and Patents Act of 1988.

All rights reserved. No part of this publication may be reproduced,
stored in or introduced into a retrieval system, or transmitted,
in any form, or by any means (electronic, mechanical, photocopying,
recording or otherwise) without the prior written permission
of the publisher.

ISBN 978-1-915048-05-9

1 2 3 4 5 6 7 8 9

Two Rivers Press is represented in the UK by Inpress Ltd
and distributed by Ingram Publisher Services UK.

Cover painting: *The Old Dairy* by Martin Andrews

Cover design by Nadja Guggi
Text design by Nadja Guggi and typeset in Janson and Parisine

Printed and bound in Great Britain by Halstan & Co., Amersham

for Ornella, Matilde and Giulia

Acknowledgements

Some of the poems in *Retrieved Attachments* are recovered and revised versions of pieces not included in *Collected Poems 1976–2016*, published by Shearsman Books in 2017. Most of them, new or revised, have recently appeared, sometimes in earlier versions, in the following places: *Axon*, *Beltway Poetry Quarterly*, *Blackbox Manifold*, *The Café Review*, *The Canvas*, *Cicatrice*, *Creative Flight*, *English*, *The Fortnightly Review*, *Journal of Poetics Research*, *Literary Imagination*, *The London Magazine*, *The Mechanics Institute Review*, *Molly Bloom*, *Noon: Journal of the Short Poem*, *Poetry Salzburg Review*, *The Punch*, *RiversSide*, *Shearsman Magazine*, *Stand Magazine*, *Tears in the Fence*, *Tokyo Poetry Journal* and *Untitled 2020*, a special supplement to *The London Magazine* edited by Matthew Scott.

'Old Kyoto Notes' also appeared in *The World Speaking Back: To Denise Riley* edited by Agnes Lehoczky and Zoë Skoulding (Boiler House Press and UEA, 2018). Earlier versions of 'Haus Europe', 'Postcards from Bern', and the first two parts of 'Dreamt Affections' were tried out in *Ravishing Europa* (Tonbridge: The Worple Press, 2019). 'From Switzerland' appeared in *Longitudines*, accompanied by translations into Brazilian Portuguese, Dutch, French, Italian, Romanian, and Spanish. 'Above the Sea' and 'Speculative' appeared in *Specimen* with Italian translations by Pietro De Marchi, German ones by Ruth Gantert, and French by Renato Weber. 'One Last Time' was published in the memorial volume *Kevin Jackson 1955–2021* (Holland House Books, 2022). 'Further Constitutionals' was written for a tribute volume presented to Sally Mortimore on her stepping back from a decade as managing editor at Two Rivers Press. My gratitude and warmest wishes go to those involved with the above, and especially to Martin Andrews, Nadja Guggi, and Anne Nolan for their contributions to this book.

Contents

Return to Sendai

Night in Nigawa | 3
Open Account | 4
The Question | 5
Uegahara | 6
La Considération du Retour | 7
Cinematic Days | 8
Shakespeare Garden | 10
Old Kyoto Notes | 11
Diplomatic Memo | 14
Tokyo in Glimpses | 16
Commuting Dusk | 18
Return to Sendai | 19
Flood Defences | 20
Street Scene | 22
Distant Visitation | 23
Far Views of Kabutoyama | 24
Hirose River | 26

From Switzerland

Above the Sea | 29
Haus Europe | 30
Postcards from Bern | 32
From Switzerland | 34
   1. Political Week
   2. Bahnhofstrasse
   3. Heute Kunst
   4. Pictures from an Exhibition
   5. Friedhof Fluntern
   6. Unterseen
   7. Unpacking
   8. Lakeside Lights
Speculative | 42

Enigmas and Environs

Spectacle of Memory | 45
The Enigmatic Week | 46
Here You Are | 47
Eternal Return | 48
The Apprentice Bookseller | 49
Global Credit | 50
Seducing the Uncanny | 51
Ghost Photograph | 52
The Three Graces | 53
Across the Park | 54
  1. Parco Nord
  2. The Mothers
  3. Presentiments of Night
  4. Black Economy
  5. Importing Love
Gasometer Music | 59
Literal Italy | 60
Interior Life | 61
Immense Prospects | 62
Perpetual Elsewhere | 63
Other Light Effects | 64
Toast Funèbre | 66
The Invidious Signs | 68
Echo of Departure | 69
The Red Cloud | 70
Variations on a Theme | 71
Via de Chirico | 72
This Other Lifetime | 74

Retrieved Attachments

Union League | 77
Via Gellia | 78
White Building | 81
At Wickenby | 82
Fireproof Depository | 84
Dreamt Affections | 86

Fashion Statement | 89
Retrieved Attachments | 90
The Revenants | 92
From the Shadows | 94
Given Directions | 96

Manifestos for a Lost Cause

A Ballad Footnote | 99
About the Lake | 100
Sheltering in Place | 102
   1. Fool's House
   2. From a Study
   3. This Last Summer
   4. Politics
Resigning the Landscapes | 106
   1. Near Heslington
   2. By Mablethorpe
   3. At Grassendale
Poetry and Money | 109
The Plague Ships | 110
Manifestos for a Lost Cause | 112
People in Fog | 116
The Last Lamps | 117
Next Slide Please | 118
Later Manifestos | 120
Toll Bridge | 122
Further Constitutionals | 123
Bird Life | 124
One Last Time | 125
Behind the Shops | 126
The Garden Path | 128

Return to Sendai

Night in Nigawa

Waiting here in twilight
while the chocolate-coloured train
clatters on a level crossing
as if the night were not so dark
because of shop-sign neon,
it's almost like there's less to fear
although the sun has gone
while still no crescent moon
can put in an appearance –
less to fear because, because
ahead each lighted window
glimmers in Nigawa pools
and warrior helmet mountain
has its pink-tinged afterglow.

Open Account

Like a Sumitomo bank account
with passbook, card and secret numbers
still working after all these years,
I'm open to the reminiscent
scents of air conditioners
on local railway trains.

Drawn upon when temperature rises
by faintest hints of drains,
I hardly credit nuanced tones
of the Japanese nightingale ...
Not born for death, that *uguisu*
sings through wooded slopes, its haunt,
like a Sumitomo bank account
still working after all these years.

The Question

Emerging from tarmac,
a solitary cherry
blossoms under rain;
from raised banks it leans
over riverine margins,
a respected elder.
Warning cars away,
they've put in red-striped posts
(captured on your phone).
Stilled as a sculpture,
look now, there's this heron
sentinel in reeds.
Oh, but I'm sorry
for yet another squabble
over such white birds.
Were they egret kinds?
As if we hadn't trouble
enough along our journey –
a sentimental one
back home, or so it seems
after these ten years.

Uegahara

Treading on the sharp-edged stones,
we'll be climbing up at dusk
by uneven, dusty steps
on what must be an ancient path
from riverside to higher fields.
Past boulders of retaining walls
to borderlands, our home,
a temporary home with houses
built on remnant terracing we come
to find their antique, foreign style
makes passing hikers pause –
and we too might hear distant pasts
as those two crows call to each other
from tousled tops of pines.

La Considération du Retour

Beside the local station platform
down drop level-crossing gates
with flashing lights, loud gongs to tell
of trains from whence the arrows point:
transparent pasts and futures come
under pantographs, powerlines, pines,
and over the whole geometric tangle
there's even a daylight moon!

Now their river brims with grasses
and the swish of water flowing
points up a quiet as near-silent cars
have drivers bowing at the wheel.
It's a quiet like nothing happening,
though here a schoolgirl cycles by
whose hair streams in the breeze
troubling those tangled pines.

A plane bank-turns below that moon.
On a walk back from the bakers
past stirring heads of yellow flowers
you ask me am I disappointed
now a black crow wings across
mocking errors through the day,
and might ask where I got my title
'La considération du retour' …

It was there on a patisserie display!

Cinematic Days

for Hiroshi Ozawa

Hollywood Spanish colonial
(as if outtakes from *Vertigo*)
is how this missionary institution
with moon's mastery serves to show
lights of self-realization
here, for example, at Number 6 West –
the three slim catalogued palms out front
and on a good day sunlit, blue
heavens are flecked with white cloud-tails
above its cream clock-tower …

and especially today
now a brighter morning shaft
focuses this sunbeam
from one curved folding chair-back
in a neighbour's garden
so that the glint of its ray
projects palm-fronds and pines
onto our living room wall
as a shadow-play grisaille –

these Hollywood Spanish colonial
groves of academe
being home, a temporary home
where tired souls in flight
might pause to reflect awhile and dream –

dream that the mastery serves to show
on a shallow, sandy floor
scabbed carp laving themselves in its flow,
you following changes of water
over lapidary pebbles to see

inside a face peeled back
another one, more blissful,
and to find old loneliness is transformed
now we've returned this far to pray
its flow wash stresses away …

Shakespeare Garden

for John & Christine

1

'No longer … to yearn for anything more'
was one of my mad ideas
where a new-born family slept
on your fresh-smelling tatami floor,
smoke plumes hung round the whole area,
odours of death remained on the air
in this city devastated only weeks before
by Great Hanshin Earthquake fires.

2

Now like a pair of shocked revenants
we tiptoe through undergrowth and stare
at where our new-born family slept,
that downstairs guestroom repurposed, too,
as the College's furniture store –
piled chairs and school-desks left behind
on its tatami floor.

3

Then through the air come blossom scents.
As if my idea were to accept
repurpose everywhere, we hear
how *les jeunes filles en fleur* would laugh,
pose, take a selfie-photograph
in the Garden of the Bard
which still has rue, has rosemary,
after all these years.

Old Kyoto Notes

'clear out of the picture'
Denise Riley

   1

Blossom time back in Kyoto
to catch at glimpses of ourselves
from the lives that were, we'll pause
while other tourists take a photo –

or be photographed ourselves
now time lived flows forever
past pain down managed levels
of the Kamo river –

   2

and where its Y of two streams merge
converging in the heat
around about mid-day,
tiny birds fan at our feet,

hawks wheel, tumble across,
a couple of crane flap by,
that egret in the shallows
takes my breath away.

   3

On awkward-turtle steppingstones
mothers with their children,
schoolgirls in uniform
leap, or dodge each other.
It's like a traffic jam.

Although indubitably here
hiding in plain sight,
being written out, or not
a part of their own stories,
you still can't disappear.

4
From on that bridge, late evening,
its lanterns orange in a night
of cloudless climes and blinking neon,
dark gulfs between each point of light
are an interstellar vacuum.

Thanks to the gravity, our airiness,
come back from a video rental
I'm firmly on that parapet,
tiny in earth's shadow, yet
head up, heading home.

5
Oh, and it's a shame
I know, being seen like this
near the flower-shop at a corner,
all its colours on display –

as if to deck a corpse or coffin,
though death might be the very last thing
on anybody's mind
this public holiday.

6
Two alien lovers kiss,
a wading fisherman
lets go his reeled-in fish

and once again I'm ravished,
cagey, but not caged –
this boy set free …

7
this boy with his own snake-belt and knees
below real traffic stuck on bridges
and that same bundle of sensations
as if stepping into the river twice

where at stirred petals' peripheries
you can almost hear the voice
of someone lost, somebody who
would take an edge off solitude
despite those great renunciations
mayflies make, or midges ...

Right now, I renounce them!

Diplomatic Memo

for Alastair & Ayako

As on an embassy out of the past,
ambassador, how you bring
further distant memories
approaching along our front-lawn path
between its speckled marguerites
and grass tufts bowing in the breeze.

Catching a breath between embassies,
with your lady wife, you bring
us news too of these present days,
ambassador, their cruel schedules,
missions, briefings, roles
that wrinkle brow and tire eyes.

How different from your current posting
is our florid scene
brimming with greenery, voices, homes
beside this dutiful Confucian river
where nobody tails or photographs you
as in bad Cold-War dreams!

How different too these tended gardens,
their singular house designs
or talking freely of our country's
sorrows, Europe and her pains,
where past grey-stirring bamboo trees
run private railway lines!

For here there's time to climb a mountain,
gaze out from its viewing platform
as far as hazed Osaka Bay –
while risen over Kansai airport
a single outbound plane
takes its disappearing roar away.

Ambassador, it seemed an echo
from intractable conflicts near
their self- and other harms
news-flashed across the day you'd leave:
they're disembodied in the shade
of respite, pines and palms.

Ambassador, could I paint this scene
with coasters, other inward flights,
PA for tsunami alarms,
I'd outline the water's edges
with couples, kids, life here at play,
reaching to that tensed horizon –

as when at Kobe's Meriken Port
towards the Inland Sea
this same horizon stretches taut
between two lighthouse piers
and straining from its rebuilt wharves,
ambassador, eyes fill with tears.

May 2017

Tokyo in Glimpses

for Giulia

1

Here at Kichijoji, like an old grey ghost
come back to haunt Japan, I'm lost
in thought: life choices, gains and losses,
deep shadow from its overpasses …

2

I'm telling the time on a borrowed façade,
the Kitte Building, and to think its remade
futurist-modern might well have come,
but for a memory of Amsterdam
in the renovated railway-station's brickwork …

3

or dusk on the roof of a low-rise flat block
given over to allotments, the greenery's
thermal insulation, its protected trees,
and a gardener at his compost
where, in fact, we're none of us lost

4

though distracted by propped trees
wearing tightly wrapped puttees
in the Imperial Palace Garden
when catching up with the moral and burden
of others' ten-year histories –
an earthquake tsunami in their days,

5

which is how we come to know
through an open bathroom window
how each Odakyu bus
has found its way back home, like us,
from the day-long wanderings

6

that took in, amongst distracted things,
being tracked down on the Internet,
a grown only child in her bank-vault flat
who would lead us up to the forty-fourth floor,
oh, that vast apartment tower,

7

to point out Inokashira Park
for once or twice around its lake
by dog-walkers, joggers, the reminiscent
swan boats' moorings where we went
to paddle them in your childhood,
look, your earnest, your relentless mode

8

has brought me here for more forceful exercise
now we talk out, we exorcise
your old grey ghosts come back to ease
or feed their fading memories.

Commuting Dusk

Darkness, here, comes fast and early.
On a limited express at dusk
as if to the *Zazie* title theme
its driver points a white-gloved finger
recognizing signal lights
and further level-crossing gates.

As on a mountain, from its summit,
dusk come, after one wrong turn
down, descending into darkness,
we'd end up we had no idea
where: a boardwalk, crest of ridges
black against the deepening sky ...

Then came a hospital with bus stop,
a bus, parked, showing wrong directions.
Whatever, we hadn't the means to pay,
as good as stepped into a past
without currency, cards or mobile phones.
Headlights would fix us, turn away.

Although we were committed to them
roads ahead all looked mistaken
as if we'd stepped into a future –
like when those friends of friends
went hiking in the Soviet Union,
but came down to another country ...

This driver's dumb show of routines
conducts us through the local stations,
illuminated fairy palaces
on fearful, labyrinthine scenes.
Just so, it took a stranger's kindness
to point our way back home.

Return to Sendai

for Miki Iwata

Beyond a rusted, padlocked gate
at Matsunami-cho
where for years I'd wait and pine,
under its branches' long wave curve
what with the Lawsons convenience store
and local supermarket gone,
it's really like there's no such zone.

Beyond the rusted, padlocked gate
at Matsunami-cho
where our flat block's since demolished,
although you say those lines of mine
have a place in the place's story,
I'm far too old to clamber over.
It's like those fourteen years had been abolished.

Beyond this rusted, padlocked gate
at Matsunami-cho
a risen sun would alter all
moving across its scuff-marked parquet,
souvenirs of elsewheres on each wall.
Here two daughters came to life,
and we played 'nothing but blue skies' in the dawn.

Beyond that rusted, padlocked gate
at Matsunami-cho
we've been exiled from our exile
under the pine wave's broken curve
and pushing through rucked, buckled asphalt
even here the summer grasses
show deep-buried traces –

like those verses of mine from some thirty years ago.

Flood Defences

1

Our boatman shows his photographs
of how things used to be
here at Oku-Matsushima
now half Japan in miniature,
it's fallen off a cliff.

That chance-made, cropped-out map
with bonsai moss-tree crust
has been eaten away by polluted air,
irradiated oysters, Chinese sand,
by all their flat-lined years …

2

Firm still on the helm, he aims,
manoeuvring his craft
into a cove of wave-curved stone,
is pointing out a green lagoon
underneath its pine-topped face.

Expert, calm, he's rightly proud of
all this natural artistry,
but veers around now, as explained,
when suddenly the offing roughens
and lighthouse island drops away.

3

He'll take us back along a seawall
newly raised against those waves.
Since the great one sucked, and came,
months on in their catches' guts
the fishermen find human hair.

His boat accelerates, slams and bucks.
It kicks against a running swell.
Spray's freshening our faces

caught amid its sculptural forces,
these exhilarated shocks.

   4
Fishing boats moored beside a mole
are jostled out along the point.
At intervals, a next bay's spume
shoots through wind-bent pines.

Newly raised against those waves,
likewise, here at Tsukihama
round its crescent-moon-shaped beach
they've built a higher seawall.

   5
Rose-bloom nets draped on old concrete,
a casual clutter of rust and the rest,
those years ago, looked set to resist
erosion, encroachment all around.

You search in vain for dreck and wrack,
tarred, tangled ropes, a crusted anchor,
house doors opened onto silence …
all swept away, its people lost.

   6
Yet how that place comes flooding back
in a borrowed house on Yagiyama
when what had rattled screen and window
starts high ripples in its pond …

Then how your poor joke comes back too –
'No tsunamis up here at Matsunami-cho …'
Yes, how it all comes flooding back
to chasten and chastise you.

Street Scene

after Shunsuke Matsumoto

This scuffed, wind-ruffled crossroads with a rickshaw
and *Canadian Pacific* offices
is what inspired my 'Corner Store'
when driving home one frozen night
we came upon a retail outlet
surviving between two corporate-finance
high-rise blocks in the business district.
Up ahead, its shopfront window faintly glowed.

Dispensing machines stood arrayed outside.
It was like a fridge door left ajar.
Not one vehicle anywhere in sight
would cross the intersection as we stayed there
stationary at our stoplight.

With a shiver, it all comes back to mind,
his *Street Scene* where we might have been
queuing outside to begin
ghost lives, our current ones gone awry
those minutes or long years before
when, stranded here, came granddad's wished-for
emigration to that farther shore.

Distant Visitation

As from beyond the grave, you write
of bamboo beating close to a window
in the season's gales and want
to hear a myriad insects trilling
long into the night.

You see again the Japanese Rhine,
see it rain-pocked all the time,
and wouldn't mind being a Japanese maple
they're so substantial-insubstantial.
But that's another story.

And on a leaf-viewing day in autumn
no photo can do justice
when among real living trees
a flock of long-tailed tits
flies down and flits about …

Then another picture: this time
it's one of the numerous islands
at Oku-Matsushima.
On the right-hand end is a lighthouse.
I'd like to be the keeper there.

It was a dragonfly-mating day.
Thousands floated past us, coupled,
and though you only get one day,
there's a lot to be said for reincarnation
as a dragonfly at Oku-Matsushima
however many lifetimes away.

Far Views of Kabutoyama

'... and if I had filled the picture with things
where would the bird have been able to fly?'

for Masanori Ito

Warrior helmet mountain at a distance,
on weekends, public holidays,
see how they traipse up from the station
in bright-coloured hiking gear –

animist spirits, a pilgrim band
with bentos, back-packs, sticks, sun-visors,
starting out from here ...

*

Just as that mad-about-painting hand
made artifacts in ripened age
to teach us how the floating world
moves beyond its image edge –

Hokusai kept changing his name,
and even tipped-up fishing craft
probably survive their *Great Wave*
remaining in its frame.

*

Those people being born at sixty,
reborn ascending, no, not frozen
on a slatted wooden bridge,
umbrellas hurried under slanting rain,

they're animated, in good weather,
like anime survivors
being born again.

*

The way those antique hikers climb
towards Kabutoyama's temple
following that torrent river!

Not tied to a memory, without nostalgia,
pasts completed, gone forever,
I'd watch them stride in admiration

on slopes of warrior helmet mountain,
would see them traipse up from the station
meaning to start over.

Hirose River

How water's flowing over stones,
fast flowing in this heat haze
under Katahira's windows …
and gone by where Ralph Hodgson's
housing was, I'm grateful for
our fourteen life-transposing years,
yet beyond its cliff-edge walls of windows
have nothing but these words for those
who kept us company …

From Switzerland

Above the Sea

In a bar above the sea at Sori,
overwhelmed by all its bay
held in the light of sensations that day,
I was gazing at sailboats, swimmers and the rocks …
You told me it's where you wrote your diary
and I thought: 'not enough
just to live', what you need's a narrative,
but then again, how give
sensations a plot sounding true to one another,
and how plait all the threads together
or leave them dangling …
Yet while the waves broke over those rocks
as momentary patterns and vortices,
I could sense in unpredictable, reiterating shocks
a way to weave the story of your love.

Haus Europe

Bluish in a white-out light at dawn,
snow blowing through a streetlamp's nimbus
was more nostalgia for our Cold War
where the ghost of a family car
hunkered beside iced-over pine fronds
shivering at an east wind's
sudden return to winter that mid-March.

But here in the Alps at an end of winter
by heaped-up strata, smutty snow,
last night a hungry deer
fed from the garden's dry grass ends
while glasses sounded for our health,
mixed dialect, language, idiom
from south and north come home …

and now this sound of distant gunfire
or – as likely – rolling thunder
is a starting avalanche
under the town band's foreground tones
scaring off its grown-up young ones,
who would be compelled to leave
resounding bands of rock, pines, chalets'
shuttered windows under eaves
piled high with layered snow.

Back then, dawn silence stunned the air,
but for one far jet-engine roar.
An inbound flight from somewhere
would be our European lovers
in need of their own place to land,
and tracks through the roadway's snow
stood out as worry furrows

on brows, them pining for each other ...
Like those who neither feel nor know,
if we can't help them live and move,
well, there again, it's time to say no more.

Postcards from Bern

1

Given my vertigo, wish you were here,
while loved ones climb the cathedral spire
and I listen to a street musician
lift the spirits higher
bringing *Recuerdos* of the Alhambra
to Münsterplatz at Bern.

2

The wood scents from a church interior
call up Scargill's V-shaped chapel.
I'm catching my breath by its graveyard at Thun.
Away across the lake
an echo of von Kleist's last cry
couldn't shift a cloud above
our young people's sky.

3

In rose-flush sunset on still whitened peaks
of the Bernese Oberland
by opened windows, looking down
from what appears like Ferris-wheel height,
thanks to Walser's footprints in the snow
or those few marks on some paper by Paul Klee,
this illuminating town
might go the distance to disprove
what Harry Lime *would* say …

4
Then were you here, as would only be right,
a balloon might rise above Monbijou
towards the Baltic coast's
beaches on that day we'd leave.
Then were you, it could well disprove
disparagements of all the peaceful arts might give
for their grown-fonder love,
oh, and these memories.

From Switzerland

'Ye guiding Powers who join and part,
what would you have with me?'
Matthew Arnold, 'Switzerland'

1. Political Week

'τὰ πάντα ῥεῖ καὶ οὐδὲν μένει'
Heraclitus

Turning for home, now, across the calm lake's
readable ripples and flows
by way of slant reeds, its turquoise shallows,
ports of call, the *Panta Rhei* makes

more distance emerge in its churning water,
lacustrine distance – you said out loud –
today's sun burning the brighter
come through a morning of banked-up cloud,

and slowly evolving from earlier mists,
the content, the contentment of these days
may still be carried forwards

over such luminous peaks and crests
with yacht sails aflutter about their stays
and reputations going, going, in so many words.

2. Bahnhofstrasse

'The signs that mock me as I go.'
James Joyce

Then towards one pavement's shadow-zone,
one after another, a grey threaded way
through *bürgerliche Gemütlichkeit*,
here the eyes don't mock you;

no, they let you be
alone along the Bahnhofstrasse,
beside Hotel zum Storchen
or the Zürichsee –

*

as if the ghosts of Emmy Hemmings,
James Joyce *in extremis* on this same street
had both struck up together

with a small guitar or cabaret
orchestra of pots and pans
au-dessus de la mêlée …

*

as distanced as the point of view
in a battle scene by Altdorfer –
turbulence driven through Alexander's forces
swarming across that filled valley floor,

the charge, the charge and counter-charge
of factions clashing in a partial darkness,
even if we're true to one another
and highhearted youth will come no more!

3. Heute Kunst

Three holidaymakers by chalk cliffs on Rügen
are gazing into a spiritual sea
or, later in the century,
a villa with cypresses, dark against waves,
it's haunted by a woman,
last scion of her family …

Then as if to mock me as they go
HEUTE KUNST is the sign I see
placarded there in red & white
on a plain, refurbished factory wall
jammed hard against your commuter-train lines …

It reminds me content carried forwards
might still sustain now the drawn-out fate
of peoples, nations, a continent
once more is obliged to wait
on resolute, resolving, imaginable words.

4. Pictures from an Exhibition

AT THE RIETBERG

for Susanna Niederer

Amongst heaped Japanese rocks, a flight
of cranes bisects their snowy-cratered,
cloud-drift mountain peak.
It leads the eye to left from right,
a vanishing point or like
its opposite, and might
have raised that pointed question:
where in a visual field would our eyes
go to find the future?

OBERSEEN

Diverted by those words tonight
on a path beside the forest edge
over their dormitory village,
its chalked-on pavement cul-de-sacs'
Achtung Kinder! signs at corners,
I scan along pre-Alpine summits
unable to be sure.

For looking must surely start from a present,
different depending on who you are –
resisting temptations to oversee
those children at play round each street fixture.

But when one refuses another's metaphor
and won't play dead, or play at all,
I stare off at the *Altstadt*'s spires
to find it precisely where young desires
coincide upon this peaceful scene
suffusing in warm, oblique dusk-light
their attenuated picture.

5. Friedhof Fluntern

for Pietro De Marchi

That'll be the day when as in a *Traum*
we took a passing trolleybus
then number 6 tram
for an unplanned pilgrimage into the unknown
outskirts of Zurich, the day when, arrived,
we photographed one solitary
narcissus poeticus flowered on its lawn …

and, memory, that'll be the evening
of a multilingual menu with deliberate mistakes
muddling cuisines, as in *Finnegans Wake*'s
gobbledygook dream-work,
laughing at world traumas and foreshadowing our own
homemade Babel from the words' *Schattenzone* …

that'll be the night when
an ill-spelt letter came giving me the sack,
my love life tumbled off a cliff-edge
no-deal withdrawal and, with travel plans in ruins,
we opted on an impulse then to stay.
Oh, that'll be the day …

6. Unterseen

Bright globes glow against an Alpine night.
Lamp-lit, canal-side, a cinder path
takes us between the Interlaken lakes.

Across its head-high railway bridges
chasing back and forth above us,
past moored gaudy pleasure steamers,
the racket from an express train
clatters a silence come between
that bank with gift shops, grand hotels,
and this reserved, preserved,
still village of Unterseen –

where two lit figures, those silhouettes,
are our young lovers striding on,
enisled themselves, then gone into the dark.

7. Unpacking

'Was it a dream?'
Matthew Arnold

Whether wet umbrage or red pinings,
wreckage from this later love
clutters bed sheets like a burning plain.

Their future's come to bits by way of
towels, lipstick, intimate things
mailed from bristling cities, to be home again.

8. Lakeside Lights

'Der See verschlammt, Liebe verschlammt ...'
Ingeborg Bachmann, 'Zürichsee'

Arriving and leaving, two ferries manoeuvre.
Slowly, their wake-wave's swells
fluster moored dinghies, vicinities of seagulls
riding that disturbance, while over

in Stadelhofen tunnel, full commuter trains
go clattering along their lines
towards Flughafen, Winterthur and environs
under a cloud or snow-topped mountains

where the *Panta Rhei* diminishes off that shore.
About cast shadows on Seefeldstraße's
tram-tracks, not much else sustains

love's young all or nothing at all ... Still, it remains
in the residence permits or two rail passes
from what had been promised, so promising before.

Speculative

for Roberta Antognini

Amongst those moments not to be repeated,
some weren't even meant, as when
I missed our meeting at the Bahnhof Treffpunkt
by an hour, sharp, then waited
in a café at the heart of the banking district
surrounded by everything I hated –
its polished chrome, aromas, and the scent
of money buying time, being spent
on rendezvous and assignation …

and if, embarrassed, ashamed, no longer
able, it seems, to keep an appointment,
I was haunted, a step from Paradeplatz,
by false accusations and to pass the time
in my head translated
a poem set outside Pessoa's famous café
near the Baixa-Chiado business quarter
until my elder daughter could escape
her bank desk for a moment to assure me …

then I glimpsed it, settling up to head home,
our persons both distorted in that chrome!

Enigmas and Environs

Spectacle of Memory

Brightness, unmoved shadow,
etches outlines of façades –
apartments where a gasworks was:
pink frontage warmed in stronger daylight
like an early memory, as this is,
a place to play when young
you find beyond the railway line
being dazzled by stucco in further sunshine,
and all of it seen from above and behind
sub specie aeternitatis.

*

Under a pergola's gravel-dust shade
vine leaves quiver when the trains go by.
Untroubled, they arrive and leave
with a clatter of closed shutters
on ochre plaster through those years,
years absorbed by the blank façade
like absent presences of sounds heard
between the lines in a picture-hung interior,
non-ghosts, haunting no one, still,
long since gone into that silent, airless room.

The Enigmatic Week

Thanks to that family of caravans
parked for the night beside branch-lines,
there's a relief in summer afternoons
enlivened by the lift of a dance band's tunes.

Nostalgic for names of local firms on tins,
who's tending tomatoes by pallets, machines,
the remnants of small-scale industries
long since beaten to their knees?

Here You Are

Like even those litterbins know where they are:
stencilled with the one word QUI
as if telling citizens *here you are*
(*here* across a children's playground,
here at the corner of an empty street)
while through an August's dead weight, cranes
are balancing, *here*, in the stillness and heat.
Though faded now, it still invites us
to treat these scenes as we would a home –
us scurrying like ants among salt grains
(no sooner arrived than about to leave)
when again I notice them, never that far.
It's like even the litterbins know where they are.

Eternal Return

You find an open suitcase, full of empty bottles.
It's been abandoned, disembowelled
among the roadside weeds.

Binned refuse over-spilling, there's beggary, nettles,
and all that's gone as waste, revalued,
answers to our needs.

The Apprentice Bookseller

for Carlo Ferrari

There are no statues in these squares.
Still, the whole district's enigmas,
its arrivals and departures, they return
in the form of a cast-iron water fountain
littered around with autumn leaves;
they're hardened into fact and habit
after pedestrian-crossing roulette,
the overfilled bottle-bells, refuse bins,
rotting fruit clutter left everywhere.

Off in the distance, commercial towers
have their surviving *libreria* still …
See, hereabouts, provocative signs
tighten hypermarket porticoes,
parked rows of skips, delivery points
(their packing strip for scavenging)
by moss-grown verges, loading bays –

the world's backside, a no-place else,
where its tied-off threads still show.
Those are the paths we come and go
taking short-cuts, trampled ways
past perimeter fences, curtain walls,
like carrier pigeons, revenants
with their bar-code boarding cards,
self-haunting, I won't lie to you …

and I won't lie, this no-place is
a home from home for the likes of us,
its towers, rose towers policing traces
of the profits and the loss.

Global Credit

There's indebtedness in far memories
of interviews at local banks
who outsource their own loan black holes,
banks at the mercy of small-time thieves
that get in through the sewer system:
they won't lend without guarantees
or access to a salary.

But at the dilemmas over what we'll bring
or be allowed to take away,
at clever solutions brought into play,
you can't not see their spider-plant leaves
as such a world map's air-routes
to spots we had or hadn't been
on the double page spread of a flight magazine.

Seducing the Uncanny

We live in thin air sold off by a villa
screened by one flank of its tree-lined drive.
Up on the fourth floor, where birds would soar and dive,
see, poplar leaves quiver when the branches are still.
Beyond them, suggestions of windows, a doorway
with lamp lit above it in the gloaming, we see.
Then yellow, a risen August moon gone astray
startles, complete, above surrounding greenery.
It's as if I'd invited that full moon to our bedroom
and in spite of these mosquito screens, it came
filling the new house with a quieter light
while you, quite naked in the French window frame,
silhouetted on a wall's late-modern, matt white,
had seduced the uncanny, being home.

Ghost Photograph

Unsmiling, still, three figures stare
at the lens for a family photograph.
Round studio Liberty furniture
they're set on a rug of animal fur:
a father, his up-waxed moustaches,
the seated mother, her lazy eye,
and Norma, their blonde daughter
in sailor suit, all posed before
the backcloth's painted hill-line …
See it emerge, preternaturally clear,
emanating from her mother's hair,
look now, an ectoplasmic smear,
like a flaw in the plate, a water stain,
another ancestor caught there …

The Three Graces

Now here they come, her three graces,
here to a converted workshop
at lunchtime for this needful catch-up –

and here's her paparazzo of the soul
straining to catch their meaning in his role
as note-taker for the ages …

See him jotting down love and friendship
staying to defend us with kept promises,
images, making good and whole.

Across the Park

'This half-finished park –
look, the boys attack saplings
with their sticks and stones.'

1. Parco Nord

This civic parkland on the outskirts
might be paved with good intentions.
Benches, waste bins have been set
under wall-less, wood pavilions
where rocks like bits of meteorite
are ranged down paths beyond the rows
of splinted trees, their branches
interlinked by a flounced black hose …

But if you go, you'll find low walls
already sporting sprayed graffiti,
rough-turned, heavy clods of earth
thinly sown with seeding grasses,
and there's a maze of shrubs in line
to lose you, swings, a scorching slide,
with basketball cages and everything
stood stranded as if by design …

'It's like a film-set for "the future",'
as a baby-sitter said. 'What kind?'
'Something like *Fahrenheit 451*,'
reading my thoughts, she replied.

2. The Mothers

'esiste altra pena?'
Luciano Erba

One hazy morning under parkland trees
there are children on a still-cool slide
with the mothers seeking shade,
and there's an old man in a wheelchair
attended by his spousal care
after the most of a lifetime together.

The mothers have fates in their gesturing hands,
saying our love was a fire of straw …
Yet here you are, offspring on swings,
gambling against long odds and, farther,
their hands feel the air for an emptiness, find
earth turned over, demolition works
in progress, look, and a family at distance,
the children begging to be taken home
where nobody sleeps or returns.

3. Presentiments of Night

But you don't cross the park at night.
Stones, trickles from its low canal
have brooded, stubborn waterfowl
emerging from a culvert. Grey slime
smelling like untreated sewage
splits in two these preserved green pieces
where locals hurry, stroll in daylight
or pause upon a planking bridge.
No, you don't cross the park at night.

There, come darkness, Vespas' beams
scan across those shadowed places,
lit globes in the laurels of deeper leaves.
They're pointing out towards waste spaces
where, for weeks, parked cabs align
and infants, children still not gone,
are strolled in pushchairs, wide awake,
down towards the *Works in Progress*
with no end of things to be done.

A few of the trees have plainly died,
and parched leaves tell their story:
how, in the worst of August's heat,
all council watering was denied.
But then the dusty swags of hose
glistened once more with droplets,
formed puddles round the sapling roots
in a change of mind or heart …

Switchboards phoned like dripping taps caused
that change, and on North Park we paused.

4. Black Economy

No, we don't cross the park at night.
The darker figures on street corners
are dealers with their bikes, their phones.

Arrived here from the far migrations
they haunt arcades of a Penny Market.
'But who buys?' – I ask you – 'Who supplies?'

5. Importing Love

Tomato plants, melons, the courgette flowers
in rows are bordered by a file of trees.
Their knotted trunks and coppery leaves
make screens for flat-block speculations.
But neither of us has been saying a word
about departures, returns, no, nor how hard
importing love can prove to be –

what with the never-ending customs checks,
the language frontiers struggled across
and how much it costs to get over a border,
hard or soft, though we each tried harder
than anyone ever expected and found,
surviving, how a sound grounding in pain
might prove the only way to love again …

But in that apartment block's lengthened shade,
reliving how the promise of love deceives
and – nobody's fault – will abruptly fade,
patiently attending through an August's heat
I couldn't miss then, wide-planted apart,
how two of the neighbouring trees
had reached their wind-blown tops together
and interwoven their red leaves.

Gasometer Music

Whereas in this city,
a deserted square at lunchtime,
there might be pigeons round its fountain,
leaf-shadow mottling the stone,
there might be, on the air, a student
practising cadenzas,
chord cascades, Rachmaninoff,
and might be love-names scored in benches'
time-signatures of scratch or stain –
here in our vicinity
a ring-road's lifting traffic over,
not far from the Madonnina
afternoons will wash it clean
of any sound, sense, or sensation
and beyond a depths of sleep
another deep remains unfathomed …

Echoes from gasholders singing,
they're enough to put you off its scent!

Literal Italy

Look, now, how one anonymous tree
(pollarded with leafed, thin branches)
pushes out at fiercer angles
from a rampant stump gone grey;
it's here each morning at the glass,
a kitchen door, roo-coo of doves
and brick end-wall for scenery.

Those violet-grey doves flutter
up through vinous leaves
trailed across a green mesh fence,
a line of barbed wire on its top.
Daily this happens, and a stray cat
limps by on three legs as chance
would have it, without a drop
of memory or aura or even sense.

Notice, at the tree-trunk's base,
how a plastic garden chair
hasn't been sat on for some time:
a bath upturned, the building gear,
and you are grown familiar, bare,
as if the view from a kitchen window
were all the panorama left here.

This August stillness has its day,
another round of ripening grapes
and green chestnuts upon us
in a literal Italy, as I say.

Interior Life

1

The curtains flapping at a window frame
interrupt oblique sun rays
from this summer dusk, the sky's
semaphore in a room's high corners
darkening shadows, wrinkles under eyes,
as if a sense of depth were made
not by the damage time sketches
but simply alternating light and shade.

2

It's a moment not to be repeated.
The light of this 8:30 sunset
slants across our profiles seated
round a dining table, their secret
histories, not cultivated
by tired eyes, no, all you're fated
to be left with when we lose
enlivened cheeks one of these days.

3

It falls upon two photographs
of those who die again the instant
any flushed face recalls them alive.
A houseguest in their history,
I glance around the shadowy spaces
at swallowed phrases, distances
between, you, me, and the others here
a few feet from us stretching back like years.

Immense Prospects

Repairing where an old world was still stored
we were sheltered out of life's main force
amongst poor daubs, musty tomes and worse
furniture to be restored …

Though the leaves would press their points here,
none of those objects tickled our pallets.
Hitting cracked skylights, hail's ice-pellets
pattered on flaked varnish and veneer.

*

Perhaps that smell was the chlorophyll
released from greenery in need of a rinsing,
mingled, perhaps, with dust stuck down
now earth lay dissolved by rain.

Our summer it seemed had found an ending
in the cracking of a branch outside
and in those splintered boughs tormented
by a storm's incessant winds.

*

Round by a terrace French window fixed open
against oppressive heat, the deep sky,
I stood still fathoming how change can happen
seeing as it's not too late to try.

Yes, it seemed the newly charged, the scented
atmosphere itself had changed our minds.

Perpetual Elsewhere

1

Yet darkening, closing with shorter words
at kiosk, bar, dry-cleaning outlet,
routine's features can't but tell
how our faces just don't fit
and the sense I shouldn't be here,
have overstayed the season's welcome
litters chestnut boulevards –
their diseased leaves bidding us farewell!

2

Forgive me. Forgive me my dismay
if I don't have a good word for them,
if I seem to have fallen out of love
with leaf-strewn avenues after rain,
an arcadian temple and football team …
These are the terms of disengagement
given a broadest hint from autumn
and, besides, it's time we went.

Other Light Effects

'die Syntax kreuzigen
auf einen Lichteffekt?'
Ingeborg Bachmann

Pink-streaked, these pallid-blue early dawns pierce
through shrivelled leafage stirring
on our courtyard's Lombardy poplars,
illuminating russet remnants
gusted, tumbled over grass.

They reach through the shutters to still lives
surviving with candle, nutcrackers
and a yellowed *Gazzetta di Parma* that opens
on this Christmas morning.

*

Now Apennine profiles appear at a distance:
backlit, heaped up cloudbanks
give us a momentary stay
as rose-touched Alpine peaks just go
to show the plain's extent –
revealing its prospects like never before.
The firm colours form in bright air.

Still, here, long shadows from a winter sun
proffer relief as I'm waiting, absorbed,
somewhere between 12:30 and 1:00.
I'm watching a dog lift its leg to a waste-bin
then lap fountain water and leave,
leave us here in our doubled dreams of home …

*

Knowing only too well it's time we were gone
as remain is no longer an option,
I'm wanting impossible outcomes, to stay

where holm oaks take us unawares,
their gnarled boughs on an off-white ground,
and brown-tinged, pink camellias
stand up against a mist.

Then from the ridge scree-falls emerge,
a vantage-point as whiteness
becomes this blank cloud-sea.
We're cut off by a Channel in the valley
and laurel too, red-berried holly
are fast while glasses celebrate years
like that stirring of our poplars' russet leaves.

*

For that was the colour dawn gave to those leaves
here in Emilia, as she would remain,
her co-ops, her partisan memorials
high on street corners, in graveyard or square,
and her promise of underground streams only gone
into hiding, away from inopportune times,
emerging – you'll say –

to disarm blighted distance, despondencies past,
and urge a resistance, mock leave to remain
in the lost air confounding our stay.

Toast Funèbre

Like a canvas I'd have painted years back now,
your local glass works suddenly appears
emerging from blank distances.

On this side of the railway tracks
a remembrance, as from drawing boards,
it aggravates agoraphobias,
the factory set to become a museum.

And above yet more of the signature graffiti
Bormioli Rocco & Figlio
here on its brick-dust-coloured face is
rendered in crisp, cursive script
like a welcome – as it would be – to the town.

Nothing as far as two rusted, tall chimneys
with walkways round their metal tops
stands clear across those emptied spaces.
Shadows lengthened on broken earth,
they're bold, still, against an evening's cloudless blue.

Then branch-line points lead on to nowhere
or disappear in undergrowth.
For here there are the changed perspectives
opened up by demolition,
disorientating what survives.

Left half-dismantled for a monument
to this district's industrial past,
abandoned, now it's doubly so
as its mass is revealed by a new roundabout –
access for yet another superstore.

But no, those tracks lead to this remnant,
skeletal now, of their first factory
where its silicates would be blown ...

and awe-filled, beyond the hollowed-out shell,
past signs for PERICOLO from falling things
with sky a hot glow through the vast, smashed windows,
let's raise our beakers of your winking red wine
towards that dusk horizon!

The Invidious Signs

From our side of the railway tracks
out to districts where this city
shows intent, expensive features,
avenues' azure road-sign arrows
for Milano, Brescia, Mantova, La Spezia
would leave me in their quandaries –
placenames promising a continuity
which couldn't be, the distances given
with destinations withered if I even
thought of choosing them …

Later, through an August's dogdays
on their shady sides, I'd venture
out to streets and boulevards
wanting to be you, exogamous couples
who'd chosen here for your own reasons –
would envy you the games of cards,
pastries tasted, middle seasons,
fogs, complaints, the local irritations,
even your sometimes ill-lived years
for our passed-elsewhere ones.

Echo of Departure

That house-front at the roundabout,
it's a russet pink soon after dawn,
and looks abandoned at the sound
of travellers' bags dragged over asphalt.
We have covered so much cracked ground.

Now see how departure, echoed to a fault,
has turned the stucco unresponsive
like imported feeling, unrequited,
the new developments slighted.
It's as if they felt not loved enough!

The Red Cloud

But coloured by rays at their most intense
we've got to leave, we have to fly
as swallows tumble commas through a flushed sky

(and rooted affections, a longing to distance,
train timetables, the wide-body planes,
commingle in our veins).

Variations on a Theme

of Bill Manhire's

Italy was at the seaside
or high on a mountain,
it was backgrounds of cicadas
interrupted by late traffic,
bar-staff pulling down their blinds …
and in Parma, August-empty,
left to the *extracomunitari*
(such as we'd soon be),
Africa was on the pavement
shouldering her baby
with a bright-print swatch of cloth,
Africa, and Asia too
queuing for nationality …
Someone messaged from back home
asking how was Italy?
Bill, that's when I thought of you –
for Italy was at the seaside
or high on a mountain …
True, Italy was something else,
and something else again.

August 2019

Via de Chirico

There on the front of a number 8 bus
in via Venezia coming towards us,
that metaphysical destination
gives me a shiver, a start, and I ask you,
'Where is via de Chirico?'
supposing it somewhere on the far side of town;

but as it veers left at the lights to via Trento
you're coming back with: 'I don't know.'
Intrigued by enigmatic directions
now as the bus trundles on
through a luminous dusk for the station,
I can imagine it, though,

in the spirit of that structure's saved façade
caught by honey-coloured sunlight
when, however warm pale stone,
the frontage resembles a hollowed-out shell,
a charm against split-level extension,
while day has grown theatrical

staging encounters with gloves, fruit, biscuits,
as manikins from the lit shop windows
point at Garibaldi in his square;
and the same bus diminishes towards a curtain wall
where dusk light shining up behind it
promises a late, postponed arrival …

It conjures a three-quarter moon above Parma
in pink-tinged sky the pantographs strike through,
then more masked figures at a distance,
goods train wagons disappearing
down tracks raised over roofs in the town;
and as they do, the fact of things

confirms your residence here among them,
the schoolkids biking home
by way of such small factory remnants
as lengthening shadows sharpen, redefine,
and our metaphysical destination,
it looms from this end of the number 8 bus line.

This Other Lifetime

for Ornella

Green shutters open on an early sky:
in the Casa Divina Provvidenza
even its room doors, closing, breathe a sigh.

With time, heat would release your love,
till evening's fresher breeze,
then starlight, the companionate,

and talking on a phone, you see
her hurry towards our rendezvous
beside Mazzini's statue in the square:

an open face, still trusting as you like,
enlivened with enthusiasm,
unfazed by time and, no mistake,

that's the zone from where all this life came.

Retrieved Attachments

Union League

'Chicago cradles it
in ice-green glitter'
Roy Fisher

for John & Diana

Paused by the vast, ice-green glitter you sense
at a Lakeside Drive's eight-lane-wide crossing,
economies of scale down by Lake Michigan –
a high-rise Pandemonium cradled on the night.

Ah, but in broad daylight
and inside The Loop,
these poets' conversations
are quieting their wives …

and like pretty rooms at the Art Institute
or paired Souza bands marched in opposite
directions, both playing their different tunes,
that's how it went, the Union music of our lives.

Via Gellia

'A morte é feita a curva da estrada,
Morrer é só não ser visto.'
Fernando Pessoa

i.m. Roy Fisher

Come to the Party

Setting the table for a cold-cuts lunch,
I placed one chair too many.
You put it down to my two faces,
selves, whatever, both of me
wanting a presence at your feast.

Likely. But that chair was also
for the others, yours or mine,
who couldn't make it, were delayed,
partakers of our common fate –
the absent ones, the late, for whom,
hapless, a place had been laid.

A Man Could Stand Up

but only with the aid of that contraption
lifting you out of your pharaonic state,
and daily carers who would move you
from chair to bed, then back again.

There now, you're taking me through
Joe Sullivan 'knocking the bejabbers'
from 'Squeeze Me' on *Jazz Casual*.
Asked to play it, Joe just says: 'Can do!'

Well Head

Being nourished by the dead
who keep us company,
there, at a well-kept well head,
wind-buffeted, now I see
how the waters disappear
underground to re-emerge
years later and, come here
to this sun-struck village
bowled through with crisped grey leaves
torn from stubborn trees
on skylines, I can trace the graves'
lichen-deep asperities.

A Sudden Toast

Mildewed branches in a window frame,
I see them, come back to the party,
now one of our own stands up, glass raised,
invites those gathered to remember
another from our number
whose death had brought us back together …

Then with his words there came
a cardinal compass-point weathervane
aslant and, no ghosts in your house,
Four Ways, past Glutton Bridge
beside the springs of Dove.

The Manifold

As now, though spring is here, a hole
appears in the landscape like a gap
to squeeze through, opens up
between grey walling capstones –
recompense for your last gasp.

Daylight's lengthened shadows
are pointing to a presence
in the Manifold's many-fold colours,
all of them awoken, startled,
by light effects' unbroken blues
along bud-tinted branches.

Your Garden

Driving the Via Gellia again
fresh darkness round each corner
leads us into them, alone,
then we're as quickly gone.

You've taken a leaf from your garden
leaving home, as on a skyline
branches caught in the curving screen
form a crosstree skeleton –
a hair-like profile backlit by the sun.

You've taken a leaf from your garden
languishing, ravished by daffodils,
and, Roy, got clean away.

White Building

for Paul & Maya

Between still life and low relief,
the squared off, plain, distempered walls
of Japanese size, I'm up before
there's need and tentatively slide your bathroom door ...

Here in this machine for living
with its rectilinear forms and functions, its ocean-liner curves,
practically on tiptoe, I grasp a D-shaped handle
and pull in search of breakfast tea ...

and I glance from a minimal kitchen window
to see, all in a moment,
feathers discombobulating natural leaf-shapes
on Lawn Road.
         Then,
where a Belsize Park dawn's peace and silence
hasn't yet woken its name-haunted street,
I make like a farewell to the modern
clicking your front-door shut.

At Wickenby

i.m. Mairi MacInnes

Desynchronized, four Merlin engines
heard through local childhoods
and the camouflaging woods
come back with mysterious constructions –
flaked brick choked by undergrowth and, Mairi,
that's when I thought of you
returned to your air-station now the view
from a watchtower's second storey
eases across its surviving crossed runways
towards dispersal zones;

and I thought of your whole generation's
long grief-stricken gaze
at more than a thousand airmen gone
from here to burn out German cities,
the big one, then, through flak-flecked skies,
those chalked up 'failed to return'
despite the camel-hump corkscrew roll
laden Lancasters would make
to fend off *Schräge-Musik* –
and thought of your own flyer's fall.

To glance at one WAAF's shockingly small
uniform jacket in the base museum,
Mairi, and to think of them
ranged on hard standing, cracked concrete
round a remnant Nissen hut
or rusted, antique petrol pump –
become a POW camp
(here too some stayed behind and met
life-mates among the pacifists
and land girls at Holton-cum-Beckering);

I'd good as glimpse them beckoning
across tilled fields, as love outlasts
even combat nightmares
like those you wedded, babe in pram
pushed past the rubble on Kurfürstendamm,
a poet near silenced by cares
and motherhood – although you'd gone
to plays, direction: Bertolt Brecht,
for that big city lying wrecked
in its still not walled-off Soviet sphere.

Mairi, how I have thought of you here …

Fireproof Depository

Not ten years gone, the sight
of Rembrandt's 1669
Self-Portrait at the stairhead,
a bankrupt's battered pride,
would bring him back to mind.
Displayed through a long retirement,
that was going to be my cover,
an image with great concrete structures
in desperate states of disrepair
like ones we'd rounded on a beach,
that dome-like rocky coastline
'somewhere in Sicily' or maybe southern Spain –

which is how it would all start up again
in an estuarial, a riverine dreamscape:
on elevated railway journeys
through close-packed heavy industry
we'd shoot past shipping, oily waters,
with all the speed, the overflight
of a sea-level camera towards cloudy night …

Port Sunlight! A lurid yellow dusk
come down behind my father's forehead,
no, that was going to be the cover
(if the copyright holders hadn't asked too much),
its chiaroscuro of gravy-browning
and salad cream from which emerge
his wearied, glaucous, understanding eyes.

He had parked a lifeboat in the drive.
Back home from pastoral duties,
look, in our kitchen, smiling despite
late illness, back pain, fret,
he's drying the dishes or, see, he's
sighing over his Sunday paper

spread on the living room floor, a quiet
posthumous kind of existence –
surviving in others' memories,
and as if he really hadn't died,
was driving, still, round Merseyside,
if its image hadn't been denied
this was going to be the cover.

That's how I dreamed my father, still alive.

Dreamt Affections

'*We've* done some of it. You and I and "Europe".'
Henry James, *The Ambassadors*

'Never and always.'
T. S. Eliot, *Little Gidding*

   I

In a bleak July or washed-out August
jet-lag morning, who could she be
coming from that shadowed dreamscape
to start and startle me?

Who *is* she with those collages,
a perpetual other woman,
still the same, and recognized,
though this time she has changed her hair?

An artist? Her *Merzbau* exhibit's
mounted like a low relief
altering as it's gazed on now
out of the jostle at a private view.

Has she been modelled from the life –
but composite? Somebody lost?
Someone I had to say goodbye to?
Or is she from that other England?

A country welcoming of strangers …?
We plan to meet. She'll disappear.
Then I'm left here to find her
in a washed-out August or late bleak July?

2

Arranging to meet at another private view
she's here again, the love of your night
in a scrambled Amsterdam, an Otterlo,
intent on bringing our brief affair to light.

Unpredictably often, this old love comes
back as her series of glimpses to blame you,
blame you for their fraught extremes,
then, out of Europe, she'll defame you.

Like last night, no, not united in heaven,
she and her clan were explaining how even
one reason's enough – fair enough, now – to shame you.

But still, as a cooling tower's up-plumed steam
joins its cloud cover, she'll claim you,
come over such distance to meet in a dream.

3

Then suddenly she pins me down.
'You still won't let me go,' she says.
'You're just like Goethe
murdering his daughter …'
though maybe only for the rhyme.

And I think: could she have meant Rilke?
'But no, it's you won't let me be!'
I tell her: 'Like false memory,
you fill my dreams, time after time,
with accusations hardly just.'

Waking to poplars, as if pixelated,
seen through fine mosquito screen
and still in night-refreshened air
I miss her, she alive somewhere,
inside me somehow like a friend –

oh friend, neither well-loved nor well-lost!

4
A sunset over golf-course divots
is picking out the debris –
that demeaning scenery …

With her perfume, bare armpits,
'You love me?' she asks now and I,
I'm too flummoxed to reply.

Fashion Statement

for Matilde & Giulia

Despite a chilly start, this April
still draws out its pastel flowers.
Whitethorn or the cherry, still,
enliven winded steps of ours

by concrete wall and pavement's grey
(we're making for our rendezvous).
At a corner table, expecting you
on this nondescript, humdrum day,

casually, now, just above street level,
I watch it cross the window frame
in urban drab, direction of travel
eastward past the British Museum,

a slate-toned pigeon come tumbling by
materialized out of our overcast sky.

Retrieved Attachments

Imaginary Portrait

That cream Formica table surface,
plates with flakes of pastry, cups,
a poorly printed anthology between us
were stage props in your narrative
of fluid gestures, sullied things.

Set against grey-aperture façades
opposite, an intervening street,
its traffic dust, grime, hot summer haze,
your face's depth shaped an open window,
lips moved by moving words.

Travel Writer

Inwards, the ordinary things
of life you seemed to praise
in a depth of night, Havana,
its dollar shops and shortages
realized in that haze.

Helpful, you supplied the need
and want friends pressed upon you
being moved to laugh or pity,
later, anger at the manner
your travelogue was travestied.

You Too

At hesitant words, elusively opaque,
I saw the London daylight deepen:
expecting to be strangled there
you too had let it happen,

now let your violated body speak –
which, wanting, so unsettled me,
whilst tolerance of his mistake
also lay behind your look.

Being Earnest

Remember, all that we could say
when, kneeling, I proposed to you
and kissed, embraced you in that play.

The shame you knew, it was a shame,
your face's depth in an open window
accepting of its wooden frame.

The Revenants

for Susan Garzón

While that nervous, young Alsatian
loudly leaps up at its leash,
the children kick through heaps of leafage
here in Russell Square Gardens

and, chilly, as this season turns,
we're talking, talking alienation –
everywhere now in unforeseen returns
to these divided islands …

*

or there again at Little Venice
on a bench in Rembrandt Gardens,
we would watch the barges slide
in and out of Browning's pool.

He'd come back here, that widower-poet,
from grief in Italian exile, restored
to this landscape of the novel
after their years abroad.

*

April here, you still recall
that place, a Patisserie Valerie,
where I had seen your portrait framed
in the square of an upstairs window frame.

Look how the cake-and-coffee chain
survives despite its balance-sheet fraud,
and after all those other losses
from our years abroad.

*

To think of us sitting down again
despite an undelivered card,
your letters, or my changed addresses,
each well-meant, unread word ...

We're covering such distances
where *campesinos* or *guerrillas*
have threatened a foreign wife, her son,
in glimpses from your years abroad.

*

And to think of us sitting down again
as if it had been their misfortune –
cross-border migrants' wads of money
become mere paper souvenirs,

those people sleeping by a roadside,
the FARC peace deal abandoned ...
would bring you from those silences
of our years abroad.

*

Just look at us sitting down again
to gaze a while at Beauchamp Lodge
where two young people slipped back home
that September that brought the pain ...

It astonishes the water's edge,
and you too, near a miracle,
come from your Colombia
after all these years.

From the Shadows

'mit Schmerz im Ausruf'
Rainer Maria Rilke

No need to look back, she's gone on ahead,
a darling wife, fond faithful mother
emerging from the grove –

so bright it good as half annuls her,
far sunlight up along a ridgeline
flaring round the blown blonde hair;

and there she's walking with her daughter,
another shy or haunted figure,
a wraith, to tell the truth.

        *

The truth is hard to tell or follow,
let alone think round with care
now deer are paused by lengthened shadows,

someone points out it's a hare
freezes, attentive, in the meadow's
shower-deepened grasses

and the truth is light has thickened:
it's like we're turned to salt behind her,
turned to salt or stone …

        *

Then with these later lightning flashes,
over-charged, the evening cloud
forms a darker band above us.

Its many-thousand strikes keep coming,
momentous signs as if
to ease such pent-up feeling

and pine-fronds reach out through the blue,
flaring and flared-up once again now
by that orange glow.

Given Directions

to Peter & Andrew's

Beyond Rodi Luigi's Italian café,
legendary, its name the same
though under new management, right,
we turn and find a terraced street
of planes trees with their mottled bark
like Wehrmacht camouflage …
Then, left, comes one of silver birch,
the Warner houses' monogram
and every frontage customized,
while a bottle-green pub has adverts, still,
straight on through labyrinthine routes,
us given directions that first time.

But what will have come over me
below your local railway bridge
when past a lock-up garage
someone at work on his motor
tested the starter, which shook
convulsively under its hood?

On the road to take for Hartington Road,
it had to be remotest things
familiar once, unexpectedly back
by the railings of a park,
grassed agoraphobic distances,
street names where the road-signs mark
how stubborn survivals show
not that far from Blackhorse Road
and Rodi Luigi's Italian café,
legendary, its name the same,
which we had revisited on our way.

Manifestos for a Lost Cause

A Ballad Footnote

'that little tent of blue'
Oscar Wilde

    1

We're driving east in the winter sun,
its rays, a reddish yellow dazzle.
Reality testing, phenomenal,
they're splayed about the far horizon

and cast on walls a leafless shadow.
Up ahead, the gibbous moon
rises above built-environment neon
waxing in that tent of blue …

    2

Then round the perimeter of Reading Gaol,
I make out by its locked front entrance
on an agent's board the words: FOR SALE.

But whether, behind, that remnant glow
or ahead this pallid, chilly distance
weighs and finds us wanting, I don't know.

12 December 2019

About the Lake

'The bliss of what?'
Elizabeth Bishop

This morning towards the misted lake
I'm drawn by early navigations.
Light flickering on cygnets, swans,

a mandarin couple or that coot
brood's sudden balls of soot
break into our condoned excursions.

A blackbird with its yellow beak
on the bush just inches from me
sees, but doesn't stir.

       *

A tawny brown Egyptian-goose pair
stand one-footed on the low brick walls
strangely set here in thick grass;

they oversee their seven fledglings
(who risk this lakeside path)
and keep an eye on us,

yes, and a distance from our species,
like for instance that grey squirrel
fleeing up its tree …

       *

But scared now by our species too,
as if an urban fox, a cat,
I branch off into undergrowth

while my fellow human beings,
chanced upon, will greet us or
they'll cut you dead at any distance;

and keeping my proximities,
I'm panicked by a background thought
as if spread on the air.

      *

The one supposed to give life meaning,
I carry it with me through our day
withdrawing from the sight of others.

No, you don't see me in this garden
under cherry blossom branches,
past bluebell carpets, with the leaves'

tender greens, by tulips, foxgloves …
now I ask what bliss it were
to be in paradise alone?

      *

And is the birdsong this year louder?
Are these creatures more at home
in the places ceded to them?

Only far murmurs of rubber on tarmac
or airplane up there in bright sky
remind you of the human racket –

when a great goose pandemonium,
instant, breaks across the lake
to give us pause, this morning.

Sheltering in Place

'But I am sick of politics.'
Lord Byron, *Don Juan*

1. Fool's House

This summer morning's sunlight flickers
through leafage on the faded spines,
finds shades of greyness furring floors,
a cup, some papers left behind.

Blue patches underneath a rain front
follow flash flooding, and if age is
another country, well, it's exile
or more inner emigration.

With shame still spreading like a stain
on mottled titles, it emerges
as fierce sadness comes to dust,
no ifs, no buts, damned either way,

your nervous breakdown worse and worse
between their deadlines' tragedy then farce.

2. From a Study

Now keeping, like the tortoise, to our homes
we fret in cabined, cribbed confinement,
repairing to repair.

A piano, look here, bares its teeth,
our ancestor-worship and progeny
arranged along the top.

Stood by, you find you're alone alive
again, your interior with bookcase
flecked by sun through leaves.

Framed, these paintings, family photos,
they're background for a conference call
from our self-isolation.

But, oh, this cost of avoiding people!
Right here, three months' lockdown dust
has gathered on its surfaces.

It's like we've all gone viral now,
the social distance, inner emigration
become habitual.

Then, love, like a state-of-the-nation report,
the local, immediate, back in fashion,
that grey fur under furniture

taunts us with its inkling of where best to start.

3. This Last Summer

Dear night, fresh coolness
breathed at a dustbin, August
clouds across the moon

assuage you, housebound
from those isolating months,
come up now for air.

4. Politics

Oh, how the radio knows its business!
After news of a latest crisis
'The future's not ours' now they play
Que Sera, Sera by Doris Day.

Resigning the Landscapes

1. Near Heslington

Beyond the Retreat's high flaked-brick wall
backing into Walmgate Stray,
on impulse, through a wrought-iron gate,
I let its path precipitate me
(since access to the past would be that way)
down to a paddock, an eighteenth-century
idea of landscape.
                      Here the russet cattle crop
and drop within their nettled shade.
Sheltered from more record-breaking heat
I come upon them in a sweat,
but they don't care and let me pass
safely where paths lead around
to new-build and our old accommodation
by an artificial lake.
                      But now the sense of place
ignores whoever comes and sees
familiar prospects refusing memories,
how shame, for instance, spread like a stain
when – you remember – it used to rain
each moulded concrete building block
would look like it could melt into the lake,
though, at this distance, no one's minded to explain …

2. By Mablethorpe

You take in tank-traps, whitethorn blossom,
the cow parsley in profuse bloom
on salt marsh by a tipped-over pillbox
and after hull-down caravan parks,
see dog-walkers lead their unique strains
out along south estuary shorelines
where loneliness, out of reach, clarifies
nothing at all.
                      Its firing-range land lies
far beyond green, sprouting wheat
through which a VW would stubbornly retreat
flanked by the high shoots ruffling in waves.
This managed terrain of water and leaves
led down false trackways is buried deep,
too deep for tears.
                      Enough to make you weep!

3. At Grassendale

Beside those mildewed, quarried red-stone walls
levelling with you, no, not up or down,
I see the landscape's got to be resigned.

Our estuary's plague-infested shore,
its opened spaces, its refineries
glinting in sunlight over by the Ship Canal
or a solitary aeroplane's vaporous roar,
they're promising relations before us and beyond
as down along the esplanade
gulls' signals travel not far inland
over stranded flotsam, ruddy mud and rocks
(still, now, the pestered shore looks clean enough)
and a starboard harbour entrance buoy
has its cormorant attachment
pointing out the channel into Garston docks …

Yet because the landscape's got to be resigned
in time I see you making imagined
stetches before us and beyond
bearing all of this in mind
so as not to leave anywhere, anywhere behind.

Poetry and Money

'Is this called "Mercyside"?'
Bob Dylan, *Don't Look Back*

for Paul Lally

Flashes of seagulls' wings in sunlight
white across a heaped-up cloud,
I watch them tumbling in flight
where beggars once could freely call
at this old, sold-off vicarage –
but now a slid-shut armoured gate,
an intercom, black railing spears
have been topped with razor-wire coil …

'Beirut!' is what you would exclaim
taking in council housing stock
or weed stalks sprung through every crack
on the far side of the carriageway.

'There's a poem here,' as I speculate,
'if I could only get inside to find it …'
equally secure against thief and poet
under the bright, estuarial sky.

Still looking back over these fifty years
to Garston docks' container crane
and Wirral shore with mountain outline,
I find it on Banks Road or Long Lane
as tellers number coin in a feeling palm
this early, with that seagull's cry
at stoplights, engine noise died down,
recounting such uncalled-for tears.

The Plague Ships

'Yet how its intrigue draws us on
till, aquamarine, the trim's grown clear
and a name: RIVIERA HOTEL
in the glass of that central tower –
the scene or setting for a *noir* whodunit,
a *crime passionnel* overlooking Weymouth Bay.'
'Weymouth Sands', 11 November 2016

Six cruise ships with their skeleton crews
for a week had kept us company.
Those stack-decked, parked ghost liners
in silhouette against the sky
fade in sea-mist as a front comes through;
they're outlined in that haze
of sunlight and faint breeze
with endless murmurs of the breaking waves;
and distanced, lost when weather worsens,
they plainly shift at anchor now
as we tread the sands round Weymouth Bay.

At first we'd made out seven of them;
but then there were four, as in a whodunit,
one come back by the end of day –
and I was inclined to keep count as we went
to and from the Riviera Hotel,
its nineteen-thirties speculation
past pretence, that *noir* crime scene
or emblem for a world lost, but not well.

In just five years an awful portent
had turned out worse than our worst fears.
Its art deco frontage, coarse grasses, dashed palm trees
would turn into such allegories –
as if neighbour voices raised in anguish
one morning were what had become
of those patriots' narcissistic love.

But, trust me, whatever their far cries meant,
these liners haunt earth's human shores
from the pebbles at Ringstead or even Lulworth Cove
and especially at night, more fairy palaces,
a reddish full moon barely risen
beside them with its stripe of light
over the waves by our blue-and-white hotel
where out we would walk – I could imagine –
out towards those cruise ships on their moonstruck roads,
ah, but there's no way.

4 September 2020

Manifestos for a Lost Cause

1

Our early, near-deserted street
has limbless trunks of trees
(as if they were straitjacketed)
clustering with this year's leaves.

Care workers from the hospital
are coming off a nightshift.
I'm on my daily stroll.

Across the sun-struck flags, bereft,
are shadows, likely phantoms,
imaginary fears, our own
left abandoned in their homes.

2

There's furniture laid out on the street
emergent from that darkness.
A sign says: free to take away.

As if this were our secret change,
you see the drowning persons
whose whole life's flashed before them
every lockdown day.

3

I'm crossing in and out of those
shadows at someone's approach
and see two pigeons raise their tails
over a sleeping policeman.

They back off then, agree to differ,
while, tentative, I'm still and watch
a robin on its dust-bin perch,

retiring, now catch up-ahead
a traffic light still held on red
amidst full, ruffled leaves.

    4

In the heart of the lockdown campus
is a vast, abandoned poster –
'DISCOVER THE WORLD Erasmus +'.

The world's a bluey-greenish yonder
on that corporate propaganda
but we're not going anywhere,

    5

anywhere much beyond its lake
(yet what a time to be alive!)
and gone on past our testing centre
still not open at this hour,

look how the lakeside care home
is raked in sudden sunlight –
like merely going for a walk
could so improve our day!

Look how these twenty-twenty visions
follow us now we're withdrawn
from all our sullen offices –
the book-lined, out of reach, forlorn!

    6

The very word, yet here's a thing:
you haunt an empty swan's nest
by the sluice gate near a wood.

It's like our lives hung by that thread,
the survival of their brood,
a brood I'd counted too –
but there's no sanctuary in the wood.

7
Withdrawing, see, tree-cover opens
sky to new growth on dwarf pines,
the more sage-coloured leaves

and see, to these you are united
now that with a loser's hindsight
we're as sick at heart …

8
A chilly breeze brings this suggestion
of cloud wisps from the west, and on
a roofless lockup's padlocked door
the spray-gunned, signed graffiti says:
'Suicide is <u>Not</u> the answer' –

and it's as if those words' ghost writer
had tried it, he would let us know,
us here still in the park with seagulls
pecking at their council grass …
But tell me, what would be the question?

9
Here, on Palmer Park, historic
cast-iron lamps haunt railway lines.
I'm rummaging their moment for
when that past was intercepted.

Street views, daily routes, routines
find Health & Safety standard lamps,
and all the social distancing
sees us frayed, become untied

on this valley's southern crest
facing down toward the coast,
now time's left in alternative
futures, ones we weren't to live.

10

Their caravans corralled around
a big top on the park,
music's blurring from its tent
now a circus is in town –
clouds scudding towards an early dark,

but with that sense of emptiness
as when its upped and gone,
another groundless accusation
spreads on social media
and there's nothing to be done.

11

You find the one word 'Sorry'
stencilled on a wall
without an explanation,
nothing else at all,

and over pavement, front lawn,
everywhere,
find patterns in the leaf-fall
this dying year –

for by an empty bus stop
on the way back homeward
its Perspex screens are summed up
in that enigmatic word.

12

Then all the things you meant to do,
worlds discover, praising folly,

couldn't happen in this pause
when time would have to be repurposed,

because that future's gone forever,
a manifesto for a lost cause.

People in Fog

'The adverse weather held us in front
and the disease pressed on our rear.'
Joseph Conrad, *The Shadow-Line*

1

I was kicking through the wreckage of this last year's
blown, damp, autumn leaves
when over a stream like Ophelia's your words
'I owe you my morning tears'
came back to haunt those chastened floods.

2

Then there in that bathybic twilight
beside our barn-like church hall
(sunken as any cathedral)
I saw those people in the fog and frost
with another winter's taste, its smell,
not yet lost –

3

and recalled, though they're around no more,
not even online, through that glass darkly,
after meeting face-to-face
I'd closed my office door
on all those books, that hoarded paper,
thinking – what was once my life
will be the death of me.

The Last Lamps

'The time is out of joint ...'
William Shakespeare

Between gnarled trunks down a parkland path
along beside the low embankment
are four wrought-iron standard lamps
still burning in broad daylight
as if they're out of sync or time.

There's sun diffused through clouds above them,
and the houses still weren't here
when Brunel raised his railway earthwork.
The council placed these lamps, most likely,
for safety inside Palmer Park.
Their gleams among the arching branches
are like a Gothic nave.

I'm steering clear of others by them
when, there and then, that glimpse arrives
in a time gone rotten before it's ripe,
our misread pasts, false future come
to exile us from our own lives.

Next Slide Please

'... and in what seems
capricious sequence.'
Roy Fisher

After a further pandemic
of news about vaccines, I take
a brisk walk round the lake
and find its paths impassable,

their margins trampled wider,
find this same Egyptian goose is
billing in the sodden grasses'
trodden remnant ice.

*

No, not following the science,
data theatre, only common sense,
a frightened fox, red Reynard,
darts between two privet hedges.

After a year, these streets I know
where thoughts settle at a wall's foot
or in treetops whose woodpeckers
sound like far pneumatic drills.

*

Likewise, I slip past the traffic-
light at the end of more roadworks
noticing this present tense's
counterfactual memories

as if to elegize the day –
a day turned into exercise
books of modelled prophecies
and no one giving way.

*

Snowdrops' fresh tears wobble
under sudden gusts while
in the perishing air above,
look, there, a solitary vapour trail.

Then, next slide, please, see flakes of snow
blown across a misted window
where – like the number blizzards –
they tumble, melting now.

Later Manifestos

Homeless Thought

A last truck parked on standing water,
surface run-off, gusted leaves
drowned in overflowing drain pools:
nothing's only good or bad,
think what you will, and nothing unalloyed

for thought here in its homelessness …
It follows beaten paths through woods
yearning to be somewhere,
to be somewhere else.

Upper Redlands Road

As an old dairy with compass-point vane
and moss-encrusted roofline
recalls when downs were farmland,
now, thoughts' local haunts,

they're going where your feet decide
to gasometer and Chilterns
picked-out 'in these gin-clear skies'
as a weather person's words would have it …

Feeding Bird

That white mansion, Caversham Heights,
old Cold War listening station,
it comes clear right across the valley
here from Earley Rise.

In earlier, raking sun displayed
red berried branches, twigs,
each with a droplet on its tip,
stop me, like a feeding bird
attracted to their catch-light pearls.

Parenting

Likewise, brickwork's moss-humped capstones
cut through drizzle, mist, miasma,
as what once seemed definite

(that exercise, those distances)
is pointed at routinely now,
vanishingly faraway –

*

like the whole of a life intimidated.
Look, a mother coot dips down
to feed her five young balls of fluff.

You scare a fledgling woodpecker.
Up it flies through chilly air
where thought might find a home.

Buried Country

Then, daily, on these built-up pavements,
over cracked, root-buckled flags
I think to glimpse, as from a ridgeline,
the landscape's reconfigured views,
well-hidden, buried country,

country before us and beyond
this parenthesis, still open,
its minute slice of time.

Toll Bridge

'Question on question.'
Edwin Muir

1

On the white wrought-iron curve at Pangbourne,
a toll bridge with its barrier down,
that day I stood and waited
fearing to topple in the turbulence below,
had felt a sudden vertigo
what with the few masked figures up ahead
blocking our way in a dazzle of sunlight,
each wind-gust-flustered silhouette
fringed by its own halo.

2

Then how long we hesitated on our winter's day
while, finally, they got their deal
and despite the pang, pang of remorse
at thinking how much worse
it might have been, and ought to feel,
in a moment of unsteadiness
I clung on to that parapet
embarrassed at the thought of it ...
of what's yet to pay.

24 December 2020

Further Constitutionals

for Sally Mortimore

Blossom's streaming from that cherry.
Just so, the magnolia moment
brings violet, white clouds, pallid pink,
good grief, to the gardens
and brown-tinged, flame-like petals
(intravenous bruises colour)
are littering adjacent pavement …

A thousand miles in this last year!
These mornings early as I can,
hitting the streets round here
finds me back where I began
and after a twelve month of avoidance,
well, tell me, what's the chance
of being, if I'm honest,
close to people once again?

Feet of clay, soles near my heart,
I note the masks by gutters,
masks appended onto boughs,
others trampled in the dirt,
ones worn with nose protruding
or lowered like a necklace
for these carnivals of every day …

A thousand miles in this last year,
masked too, see me advance
to glance across our own Thames valley,
at daffodils beside the lake
under an overcast sky,
or amongst the social-distanced,
anonymous passersby,
startled, in this common place
to chance upon, with family group,
your recognizing face.

Bird Life

for my daughter

Giving way to a mother and child-in-arms
on one of those daily excursions,
I might be helping reclaim the streets
perhaps, but not the night,
Giulia, now your planned
vigil on Clapham Common has been banned
under their pandemic regulations ...
I'm on the park in daylight and a world of harms.

Those Egyptian geese with their single chick
are honking at a large brown rat.
Another pair with brood of four
have lost one I counted days before,
worried how many of their five
would in the end survive.

And nor can I help fearing for relations
still not home now darkness falls
when over this ruffled lake's surface
one clattering, great-winged swan takes off
like something imagined by a Howard Hughes ...

After all these years, I'm no less haunted
by those whose power's put on with their violence
(when attentions are unwanted)
and like two lines of Zadkine sculptures
an avenue's pollarded limbs are
pleading to the skies if that makes sense.

One Last Time

i.m. Kevin Jackson

Glimpsed through wistaria petals, laburnum,
see how chestnut candles flare
standing tall on their filled-out branches,
and with them invisible forms come
round the headstones at Cemetery Junction,
startled, in plain sight.
                        Just moments before,
a noticeboard poster with photos
had shown me, no, not missing or wanted
persons, they're Green Councillors'
details for if you're in need of the council,
or some counselling.
                     Even this diminished thing,
my three-parks-walk with graveyard
you know I wouldn't be without it,
your death amongst more counted deaths
in deep-cut shadow cast by a yew
on paths to memorial corner.
                           But now
though the cars will chase after each other
again, outside, at Cemetery Junction,
I know you wouldn't be without it
especially if found now in plain sight
come round this headstone, from this quiet,
another invisible form, oh, this one.

10 May 2021

Behind the Shops

1

Then take, for instance, this short cut
with cloud-filled puddles in each tyre rut,
its gravel earth impacted,
the plastic dreck and wreckage ...
Tiptoeing through a chain of lakes
you pick out remnant signs –
O. Phillips & Sons, as it happens,
Builders and Decorators
painted on the brick.

2

Fly-tipped stuff, a supermarket trolley,
skips, bins, other far-flung gear,
they've come to rest, been retired here,
the flaking, faded traces
of long-since-failed businesses
given way to later strata.

3

Abandoned sofas on a lock-up roof!
A tyre replacement premises
has worn-thin, shed black treads
woven into heaps out back.
Look, how the world's turned upside down
as if you could already see
a future archaeology!

4

Then on the hapless, sun-struck street
like a character in search of a building site,
you see where time only half effaces
Royal Albert Garage, and the place's
proprietors: *G. Jarvis & Son
Cars, Coaches, and Repairs*,

it emerges from the smutted brickwork
in a raking light.

    5
Then, ashen, like some figure from Pompey,
astonished, you come face to face
with no world but this short-cut's back-of-shops
being history too, one of these people
who've nowhere else to choose,
no home in time than those
lived through, those infected years,
bereft, still, of our day.

The Garden Path

Grape bunches, heavy summer thoughts
in mottled shade, our futures
come at us as cherished glimpses,
hedgehog droppings, well-fed pigeons ...
Now, green-fingered, you're shoo-shooing
white butterflies off salad leaves,
and though our cabbage can't speak French
you do, love.
                Love, you do.
You're telling me how sunflower heads
are reaching over latticed fence-work,
the neighbour's borrowed scenery is
competing with our few pink roses
while by borage-sipping bees, your path
through flowers, fuchsias, leads where trellis
blackberry clusters tumble, ripened,
on our open lips.

Two Rivers Press has been publishing in and about Reading
since 1994. Founded by the artist Peter Hay (1951–2003),
the press continues to delight readers, local and further afield,
with its varied list of individually designed,
thought-provoking books.